THE ESSENCE OF
ISLAM

C.T.R. Hewer

Published by Many Rooms
Alphonsus House
Chawton, Hampshire
GU34 3HQ
England
www.ShineOnLine.net

Text: C.T.R. Hewer

Design: Orchid Design

First Printing: May 2002

ISBN: **0-85231-212-1**
Printed by: Polar Group

Acknowledgement

Anyone who attempts to write a book entitled "The Essence of Islam" undertakes a massive task: How to capture the essence of a complete way of life in only 10,000 words? When the author is a student of Islam but not himself a Muslim, then the task is awesome indeed. Before writing, the author has "removed his shoes" in order to step onto the holy ground of another faith tradition. This short book is the outcome.

This work is dedicated to my Muslim friends and colleagues, especially in our shared city of Birmingham, who by their lives have taught me much about Islam that I could never have learnt from books. In particular, I would like to acknowledge the contribution of the following Muslim scholars who read my manuscript critically and offered me the benefit of their wisdom: Shaykh Mohamed Amin, Professor Hasan Askari, al-Hajji Abdullah Bawhab, Yahya Birt, Dr Jabal M. Buaben, Maulana M. Tariq Kamal, Professor Yahya Michot and Dr M. Yusuf Qamar. In addition, I am indebted to three Christian priests, who are committed in various ways to promoting better understanding of other faiths and who kindly read and commented on the manuscript: Fr Michael Barnes SJ, Fr Matthew Joy and Fr Pat McCaffrey SSC. The responsibility for the final text is mine alone. In accordance with Muslim custom, I ask for the correction of the community and the forgiveness of God for any errors that it may contain.

Chris Hewer
Birmingham
March 2002

Foreword

It is with great pleasure that I write the foreword to this fine piece of work by Dr Chris Hewer, my friend and colleague. In a world still fraught with religious and racial animosity, any effort to present the essence of a religious faith is to be welcomed. In the aftermath of September 11th 2001, many are asking what Islam is all about. The fact that people are seeking to understand is a hopeful sign because prejudice is fuelled by ignorance.

In his present position as the interfaith adviser to the Bishop of Birmingham, Chris has established a long-standing record of excellence in working with and for the Muslim community of this city. That experience and his sharp academic insight make him the ideal person to have undertaken this work.

Current statistics suggest that Islam is followed by over twenty-five per cent of the world's population, and as Chris will succinctly explain the word itself means 'peace'. Chris has been sensitive and true to the basic beliefs of Muslims and has told the story 'as it is'. I particularly commend him for writing in such an easily readable style while not sacrificing the detail.

The prophet Muhammad lived in harmony with those of other faiths. If this book not only educates but also helps to build good relations between different faith communities it will be of great benefit to humankind. I hope and pray that Chris's work will be rewarded in this way.

Dr Jabal M. Buaben
Director of the Centre for the Study of Islam and Christian-Muslim Relations
Department of Theology
University of Birmingham, England.

Contents

THE ESSENCE OF
ISLAM

What's it all about?

"If only I could get inside your head and have a look at the world from there, then maybe I'd understand you better." That's what we're going to try to do in this short book. To have a look at the world through Muslim eyes. Now a Muslim is someone who follows Islam as a way of life, so we're going to look at life in the framework provided by Islam.

Let's begin with a challenge. How could one sum up Islam as a way of life in just one sentence? "Islam means to live a fully human and balanced life in perfect harmony with God, all other human beings and the whole of creation." That's it in a nutshell. The rest of this book is about unpacking that one sentence.

Let's begin with God

God exists. That is absolutely clear in an Islamic framework. Of course, Muslim philosophers have gone into great depth to demonstrate that God exists, but that's a book in itself. We'll begin with the point that God does exist. What can we say about God? At the heart of Islam stands the principle that God is one and there is nothing within creation that is like God. God is absolutely unique. God cannot be divided up. God does not share divinity with any human being or created thing. This is shown by the Arabic word for God, that is Allah. Allah literally means "The God". It is a word that cannot have a plural. Allah is one and cannot be more than one.

Arabic-speaking Jews, Christians and Muslims use the word Allah for God. Allah signifies that one true God who was worshipped by Moses, Jesus and Muhammad, the three great figures

of these faiths. All those who follow the ways
of life laid down by these three, that is Jews,
Christians and Muslims, call God "Allah", when
they are speaking Arabic, of course. This Arabic
word for God is used throughout the world
wherever Muslims are to be found. At the heart
of Islam stands the principle that God is one
and there is nothing worthy of being worshipped
except God.

How can we speak about God?

The world of God is beyond the world of our
human experience. We call this the "transcen-
dent world". When we try to speak about this,
all our language is inadequate. To use words
like "world" and "beyond" is to talk in poetic
language. "God's world" is not like another
place a long way away that we could get to if
only we had a sufficiently powerful rocket. It is
outside our field of understanding. We say

"beyond time and space". Everything that we say about "God's world" is limited by our earthly language and so it is bound to be inadequate. When we talk about God, which is what theology is all about, we are always doing the best we can with our inadequate language. We know that we are bound to fall short but we have to use the poor tools that we have to speak about God as best we can.

This principle is true for all religions. Whenever we start talking about God, we are always limited by language, no matter how scholarly we might like to sound. This has never stopped people from thinking and writing about God. Scholars have been engaged in this for thousands of years. There are huge libraries of books written by Muslim scholars during the last 1400 years, since the time of Muhammad. Whenever we read anything about God, including this book, we have to remember that this is only our "best shot" and God is way beyond our ability to describe in earthly languages.

To begin with God

We can only talk about God by the signs of God's actions. To begin with, then, we can say that God is the Creator who created everything that exists. God is perfect, there is no room for imperfection in God's world. A perfect creator can only create something perfect. So the universe, as created by God, was perfect. It is always in a state of change and development. Nothing stands still in the universe. Everything is always being maintained in this state of perfection or it is breaking up and becoming imperfect. Within creation, it is the role of every human being to "look after the creation" and bring it to remain in the perfect state that God intended from the beginning.

Everything is created by God, who alone has no beginning and no end. We can say therefore that God is all-knowing and all-powerful. God's power creates everything and keeps everything in existence. It's obvious that the Creator knows best how the creation should work. Who knows better the capabilities of an engine than the one who designed it? In God's plan, God has transferred some of this knowledge to human beings so that we can "tend" God's creation and bring out its full potential. This gives an incredibly high dignity to every man and woman within God's plan. Each of us is to be God's representative on earth.

Time for a little Arabic

So what do "Islam" and "Muslim" mean? Arabic is a language that is built up around families of words that share a common root. Each root has three letters. Every word that is built using these three letters is part of one family and so related in meaning. Here's an example.

Take the Arabic root **s l m**. We can make a family of three words from this common root.

islam

muslim

salam

You see the three-letter root in each word? They are related. The first, *islam*, means that state of perfect harmony with God, with every other human being and with the whole of creation that God intended and that God wants. The second, *muslim*, is that creature made by God that is in the perfect harmony indicated by the word *islam*. The third, *salam*, is the active power that brings about the state of *islam* and makes creation *muslim*. When two Muslims meet they exchange the greeting *salam 'alaykum*, which is sometimes translated as "peace be with you", but which actually means "may you come more fully into that state of perfect harmony with God that is *islam*".

Being in a state of harmony

Now if we're talking about harmony between the all-knowing, all-powerful Creator and part of creation, then this is like "learning our place in the system". It is fitting into the great design and fulfilling our destiny perfectly. This requires an element of submission, of saying "God knows best and I obey". This is part of the meaning of *islam* too: perfect harmony and peace can only come about when everything acknowledges the plan of God and enters into the correct balance that the Creator intended.

Did you notice that the word *muslim* above applies to all creatures and not just to human beings? When every element of creation is fulfilling its proper part in God's plan, then it's *muslim*. This means that animals are *muslim*, plants are *muslim*, and the physical parts of the universe, like the sun and stars, mountains, rivers and the air we breathe, are all *muslim*. That means that they all play their part in God's creation, and it is our responsibility to make sure that is so and remains so. Everything that is created by God is part of a perfect creation. This means that it is created *muslim* and in the state of *islam*. Now the sun, moon and stars, the animals, birds and fish, the trees, vegetables and flowers, the mountains, air and seas do not have any choice about being *muslim* or not. That is the way that they are created and that is their place in creation. A tree is *muslim* and that's it. Not so with a human being. God has given us the unique gift of free will so that we can freely submit to the harmony that God intended for us and be *muslim* or we can rebel against God's plan and become non-*muslim*. That is the unique dignity of being human.

From the beginning of time

Did you notice that in the last few paragraphs we were using the words *islam* and *muslim* without capitals and in italics? There's a reason for that. When we use these words in this way, there is a timelessness that goes right back to the start of creation. In this way, Adam and Eve, the first human beings, were created *muslim* just like everyone else that's ever lived. This is a bit different from when we write Islam and Muslim with capital letters. Then we mean the particular way of life following the revelation to the Prophet Muhammad and his example. Muhammad and all who came after him were of course *muslims* but they were not the first. Muhammad, who lived in the seventh century of our Common Era, did not found a new religion called Islam but rather called people back to the harmony of *islam* that was part of God's plan from the very beginning.

Guidance

If human beings are to fulfil this high dignity and be
the representatives of God on earth tending the
whole of creation, then we need guidance. How are
we to keep things according to the designer's plan
if we don't have the "blueprint" to which to work?
When guidance comes from God's world to this
world, we call it revelation. Only with the gift of
revelation can we live *muslim* lives. Revelation
comes to human beings through two sources.
One is through books or scriptures that have been
revealed since the earliest times. The other is
through studying the "Book of Creation", that is
everything that God has created. "If you want to
know what was in the mind of the designer, then
study the finished article." This means that science,
research, enquiring into the natural world all play an
important part in the life of the *muslim* man or
woman. There is no division between "religion"
and "science" in the *islamic* framework. To research
into the natural world and to research into the

scriptures are both acts of obedience and worship of God. At the end of our researches, provided that we have correctly understood them, we must come to their common source, who is the all-knowing God. Naturally, whenever we begin on any scientific research we have to work within a certain framework. This framework is provided by the scriptures so that we can test all our findings against that which has been revealed by God throughout the ages in the scriptures.

All *muslims* are ecologists

Part of being human, in this *islamic* framework, is to be concerned with the environment and the created world that surrounds us. We have no right to do violence to the creation by pollution or destroying its natural balance. Indeed, it is part of our human duty to restore and maintain that balance. All *muslims* are natural environmental scientists and ecologists.

To stop the destruction of the ozone layer, to prevent the pollution of our rivers, seas, air and earth, to use genetic science wisely in developing our sources of food, all these are part of being *muslim* and all are acts of obedience and worship of God. All advancements in scientific knowledge are potentially for the benefit of creation but must be used in harmony with God's plan. This means that to struggle against disease, to find ways to provide clean water and nourishing food for everyone on earth, and to develop sustainable forms of energy to support future generations are all aspects of the service of God and thus part of *islam*.

Accountability

With the dignity of free will and the guidance provided by revelation in the books and creation comes the burden of responsibility for the way in which every human being acts. Each man and woman is accountable to God for the way in which this gift of free will has been used and the way in which the guidance has been put into practice. At the end of our lives, every one of us will face judgement before God, who is the only ultimate judge, because God alone knows what was in the heart of the person when they performed the act. For those who are struggling to be fully *muslim*, then, this is an awesome responsibility. For those who like to pretend that there is no accountability and no ultimate judgement, then, as Muslims see it, there is a rude awakening. Each human being will have to give an account for his or her life and on that day there will be no excuses and no one else to blame or to save us from the justice that awaits us.

Guidance from the dawn of creation

God is just. It would be a fundamental lack of justice to hold human beings accountable for their actions without giving them the guidance on how they were to live their lives and thus the principles against which they would be judged. This means that God must have given guidance from the very beginning to the first human beings. In Islam, Adam and Eve were the first human beings on the earth and so they were the first to receive guidance from God. Adam and Eve were *muslims* and initially lived in perfect harmony with God and all creation. Then they made an error of judgement. They repented and were forgiven by the infinite mercy of God. Once they were forgiven, they re-entered the state of being *muslims* and so there is no doctrine in Islam like that of Original Sin amongst Christians. Adam and Eve erred, repented, were forgiven and then lived in harmony with God. Their error affected only themselves and did not have an effect on their descendants.

The Prophet Adam

Adam was the first to receive revelation from God and was charged with implementing that guidance upon the earth. This made him a prophet. In Islam, a prophet is a human being who has been chosen by God to receive a message and to proclaim it on earth both in words and in the way in which they live their life. Just as we have seen that God in justice sent guidance to Adam as the first human being, so God sent guidance to all the people of the earth without distinction. All the peoples of the earth have been sent at least one prophet who brought guidance and a way of life. Who all these prophets were, we do not know. How many of them came with a specific scripture from God, we do not know. Islam is quite sure, though, about two things. Firstly, that no people were left without guidance and so all will face judgement. Secondly, that the guidance that was sent was always in essence the same. How could a just God guide one people to live in one way and another in some other way? The essence of this message was always *islam*, that is submission to the plan of the Creator so that all may live in perfect harmony.

Two important points flow from this. Firstly, Islam has never seen itself as a new religion but as the natural way of life for all human beings to live from the beginning to the end of time. This means that when Muslims find something in another religion that is in agreement with their tradition, then this is a source of rejoicing as it is a proof that these other people are also following the guidance that was sent to them, however imperfectly. Secondly, whenever Muslims encounter new peoples around the world, then their attitude is to be one of respect for all that remains of the original guidance sent to them by God. The criterion by which all such encounters is to be judged is the way in

which the lives of peoples reflect the way of life
that was laid down in the revelation given to
the Prophet Muhammad and lived out by him.

What kind of a person?

What kind of a person is this *muslim* man
or woman who fulfils his or her God-given
responsibility of being God's representative on
earth? How can such a person be trained? This
training is provided by all the practices of Islam:
by prayer, fasting, almsgiving, pilgrimage and
correct community living. Guidance is given by
the principles of belief that are distilled from
the revelation from God. The principal source
for all this is the Qur'an (sometimes you will
find this spelt "Koran"), the scripture that was
given to the Prophet Muhammad and which
has been passed down unchanged through
successive generations. And yet correct actions
and correct believing are not an end in

themselves. They lead and prompt the *muslim* into an ever-closer intimate awareness of the presence of God, who is not only Guide and Judge but is also Friend and closer to a person than that person's jugular vein. This is the goal of a *muslim* life, to live in a constant state of God-consciousness, secure in the awesome yet compelling awareness of the intimate link between the Creator and the human being as the pinnacle of the creation.

Muhammad and the Qur'an

Muhammad was born around the year 570 CE. CE stands for "Common Era" and is the same in terms of numbering as the Christian AD. However, as AD is an abbreviation of the Latin for "in the year of Our Lord", only a Christian can properly use this. That is why "Common Era" (CE) is preferred by everyone involved in modern religious studies.

Muhammad was born to a merchant family in the city of Makka in the Arabian peninsula, in modern-day Saudi Arabia. Makka is also sometimes written "Mecca" but Makka is a better way of representing in English the sound of the name in Arabic. Makka was a trading city and a place of pilgrimage for the Arabs of that time. They were largely idol-worshippers except for a group who believed in the existence of one God only but had little knowledge about God. It was into such a family that Muhammad was born.

His parents both died and so Muhammad was brought up first by his grandfather and then by an uncle called Abu Talib. He was trained as a merchant going off on trading journeys with his uncle and his camel train. Muhammad became well respected in this work and at around the age of twenty-five he married a widow called Khadijah, who had a trading business of her own. Muhammad's character was such that

everyone knew him to be honest and trust-
worthy in his business and personal affairs.
Muhammad would have nothing to do with the
worship of idols but took himself off for long
periods of meditation. He frequently meditated
in a cave on Mount Hira just outside Makka.

He was in meditation in this cave one night
towards the end of the month of Ramadan in
610 CE. An event occurred that changed his life.
Whilst wrapped in meditation, he became aware
of the presence of a figure of light on the horizon
and approaching him. It became clear that this
was the angel Gabriel who, throughout history,
had been associated with God sending messages
to human beings. Gabriel approached Muhammad
and commanded him to recite in God's name.
Muhammad was frightened and unsure of what
he should say. Like most people at that time,
Muhammad had not been educated in book-
learning. The angel approached Muhammad,

embraced him and then stepped back. Again he
commanded him to recite. Now words welled up
from the heart of Muhammad without his being
aware of how they came. He certainly had not
made them up, nor did he have to learn them,
they were just there erupting from his heart
where they had been placed by God through the
messenger angel, Gabriel.

This was the start of the revelation of the
Qur'an, the scripture sent by God to Muhammad
as guidance for all humankind from that time
onwards. It is very important to appreciate the
Muslim understanding that it was not composed
by Muhammad but is literally the Word of God,
revealed by God to Muhammad, who was the
messenger who proclaimed it to the world.
Muhammad's heart had been purified by God
so that it would be a pure channel through
which the words of the Qur'an could enter the
world. The Qur'an made its appearance in this

way, on the Prophet's lips, gradually over the course of the next twenty-three years until Muhammad died. While it was revealed into a particular context and so must be understood against that context, its message was for all people and all times. It was revealed in Arabic, the language that Muhammad spoke, so that he could understand it and put it into practice in his life.

Not the first but the last

We have seen that Adam was the first prophet to receive revelation from God and that prophets had been sent to all the peoples of the earth. The Qur'an gives a list of some twenty-five of these prophets, twenty-one of them are known from the Jewish and Christian traditions. These include Noah, Abraham, Isaac, Ishmael, Jacob, David, Solomon, Moses, Elijah, Jonah, John the Baptist and Jesus. Muhammad saw himself standing in this line of prophets going back to Adam. He is said by the Qur'an to be the last of this chain of prophets and the seal of all that had gone before.

Similarly, the Qur'an was not the first scripture to be revealed. Earlier books had been sent to various peoples of the earth. The Qur'an gives us clear evidence of five books revealed by God but there may have been many more whose names are not known to us. These five are associated with specific prophets. Abraham was given a scripture that has been lost but is referred to in the Qur'an as "leaves" or sheaves of writing. Moses was sent with the *Taurat* (Torah), David with the *Zabur* (Psalms), Jesus with the *Injil* and Muhammad with the Qur'an. In essence all these scriptures contained the same guidance but the way in which that guidance was to be lived out in detail was particular to each prophet and each time and place in which they lived. One difficulty is that we do not have definitive copies of the *Taurat, Zabur* and *Injil*. We do have the Torah, the first five books of the Hebrew Bible, and the Psalms of David but we cannot be sure that these were the actual books that were revealed to these prophets. Christian history has no knowledge of Jesus receiving a scripture called the *Injil*, although this Arabic word has a similar root to the Greek from which we get "Gospel".

Jews, Christians and Muslims

As far as the Qur'an and Islam are concerned, Moses and Jesus were true prophets of God who came to guide people on the right path. That path is the one of perfect harmony with God and all creation, that is *islam*. In this way it is clear that Moses and Jesus, and all the earlier prophets, were *muslims*. If Moses and Jesus had been around in the time of Muhammad, then they would have recognised him as the Prophet of God and the Qur'an as the revealed Word of God. Muhammad clearly expected the followers of Moses and Jesus to recognise him after he was called to be the Prophet.

The Qur'an gives the Jews and Christians the honoured title of being "People of the Book", referring to the scriptures that were revealed to Moses and Jesus. Unfortunately, the earlier books are unreliable. In some instances, they tell a different story to the Qur'an and this makes for a big problem. The Qur'an was revealed to Muhammad and memorised directly from his lips by a group of his companions. During his own lifetime, it was written down by scribes on pieces of parchment, leather, leaves, stones and dry bones. Very shortly after his death, one definitive manuscript was made by checking the scribes' writings with the Qur'an as memorised by the direct companions of the

Prophet. This manuscript was then copied and circulated around the Muslim world. This gives us one definitive text that has been preserved unchanged up to the present time. All this means that, for Muslims, the Qur'an must be the preferred text. If other scriptures differ from it, then something must have happened to them. Either the original version was changed at some point in history or part of the original has been lost and maybe someone filled in the gap with their own words. As you can imagine, there have been some strong disputes about the authenticity of one another's scriptures between Jews, Christians and Muslims through the centuries.

Cousins in faith

What is clear and cannot be denied is that Jews, Christians and Muslims are "cousins in faith". The story begins with Abraham. You will recall that Abraham was married to Sarah but the two grew old together childless. Sarah suggested to Abraham that he should take her Egyptian maid, Hagar, as a second wife and have children with her instead. Abraham and Hagar had a boy and called him Ishmael. Then Sarah was blessed by God and she too had a child with Abraham, whom they called Isaac. Eventually Sarah grew jealous of Hagar and Ishmael and so persuaded Abraham to send them away from their home in Palestine.

Abraham was not keen on sending away his second wife and son but was moved to do so by a message from God to say that God would raise up a great people from Ishmael and so Abraham decided to do as Sarah asked.

According to the Muslim tradition, Abraham, Hagar and Ishmael travelled south through the Arabian peninsula as far as Makka. Hagar and Ishmael settled here. Abraham divided his time after that, living in Palestine with Sarah and Isaac and visiting Hagar and Ishmael in Makka. It was through Isaac that the Jewish people descended and from this people that Jesus was born. Through the line of Ishmael came the Arab people and from them Muhammad was born. Thus it can be seen that Moses, Jesus and Muhammad all have Abraham as a common ancestor and so Judaism, Christianity and Islam are cousins in the faith of Abraham.

Pilgrimage

Once each year, the Hajj or Pilgrimage to Makka takes place. This is the biggest annual gathering of human beings on earth, with an estimated two million people each year.

Muslims come from every corner of the world, from every ethnic group and speaking every language to pray together to God in Makka. The Hajj is not just a link for the geographically divided worldwide community of Muslims but it is also a link with Muslims throughout the ages of history. Many of the rites of the Hajj go back through the Prophet Muhammad to the prophets Abraham and Ishmael.

On one visit to Makka when Ishmael had grown up, Abraham and his son built a building in which they could worship God. It was called the Kab'a and stands in Makka to this day, although it has been re-built over the centuries. This building now forms the earthly focus of prayer for Muslims worldwide. Every day, five times a day, Muslims are required to pause in their work and turn to face in the direction of the Kab'a. Once in their lifetime, if they have suffi-cient money and good health, every adult

Muslim man and woman is supposed to follow this direction with their whole body and make the pilgrimage to Makka. In this way, the pilgrimage is a gathering up from around the world and a uniting across the centuries, all in the worship of God. When people go on the pilgrimage, the men are required to wear two white sheets of cloth as clothing so that all are exactly the same regardless of their social status, wealth or ethnic group. Women are required to wear a plain full-length dress. Even the clothing thus signifies the unity and single-mindedness of the Muslim community at prayer.

When in Makka, pilgrims walk around the Kab'a and pray there as did Abraham, Hagar and Ishmael. They then run seven times between two small hills to remember the desperate search for water when Hagar thought that her infant son would die of thirst. On that occasion, God provided a spring of water for Ishmael and

Hagar. That spring runs to this day. It is called *Zam Zam* and pilgrims drink of its water and bring some home for family and friends. The climax of the Hajj comes when everyone leaves Makka to go into the desert to pray on the Plain of Arafat. This is the solemn moment when all who are truly repentant of their sins are assured of the forgiveness of God. Together they stand and pray for a few hours, each profoundly alone and yet united together before God.

The next day everyone goes to a nearby place where stand three pillars of stone. This again relates to the time of Abraham and Ishmael. These two prophets were tested by God to see if they would be truly obedient in all things. Abraham was commanded by God to kill Ishmael and Ishmael was commanded to be willing to be sacrificed. Together they went into the desert to perform the command of God. On their way, they were tempted by the Devil to rebel and disobey God. They drove away the Devil by throwing stones. Now all the pilgrims do the same thing by stoning the three pillars as a sign that they will reject the Devil and the rebellion of sin in their lives.

At the crucial moment of their test from God, when Ishmael was waiting for death and Abraham was about to sacrifice him, Abraham was halted in his action by God who told him that they should sacrifice a ram instead. They had passed the test of obedience in all things to God and the life of Ishmael was to be spared. Together father and son found a ram nearby and sacrificed it to God as commanded. Today the pilgrims, and Muslims all over the world, celebrate this day by sacrificing an animal, cooking it and having a feast. This is called 'Id al-Adha, the Feast of Sacrifice. Part of each animal so killed is given to family members and neighbours, and another part to the poor so that everyone may share in the feast. You may recall this story from the Bible, but in that account it is Isaac and not Ishmael who was to be sacrificed. This is one of the disputed questions between Jews, Christians and Muslims. According to the Qur'an, it is clearly Ishmael who was tested in this way.

Back to Muhammad in Makka

Muhammad himself performed the Hajj and thus established the link with Abraham and the rites to be performed, as guided by the Qur'an. In the early years after the revelation of the Qur'an began in 610 CE, Muhammad and the small group of Muslims who believed in the message of the Qur'an were persecuted by the idol-worshippers of Makka. The early verses of the Qur'an that were revealed at this time called on people to leave off the worship of idols and worship God alone. The first Muslims were tested in their faith but they withstood persecution and gradually their number grew to a few dozen. It was also at this time that Muhammad made his Night Journey (*mi'raj*) in which he was taken to Jerusalem and from there ascended into heaven to the Court of God, where he received instructions on daily prayers. It is this association with Jerusalem that makes it the third most important city in Islam, after Makka and Madinah, to which city Muhammad later migrated.

In 615 CE, Muhammad was concerned that they might all be killed by the Makkans and so sent a group of the Muslims to seek refuge with the Christian King of Abyssinia. When they arrived at the King's court, he asked them to recite some of the verses of the Qur'an that they had memorised. When he heard them, the King recognised that this was a message from God similar to the Christian one in which he believed. He gave the group of Muslims the protection of his realm and they remained there until it was safe to return to rejoin Muhammad years later. This was the first encounter between groups of Muslims and Christians; fortunately it set a good example for later years, although it was not always such a happy co-existence.

In the year 622 CE, Muhammad moved away from Makka with the remaining group of Muslims and they settled in the city of Yathrib, some 300 kilometres north of Makka. Yathrib was renamed Madinah, which is short for "The City of the Prophet". The people of Madinah had heard Muhammad's message and had invited him to come and set up a Muslim community in their city. Islam now took on a new phase. Muhammad was faced with becoming the leader of a settled community and establishing laws by which they should be governed. The verses of the Qur'an from this period are much more "constitutional", setting the principles by which a Muslim society should be ruled. It is important to note that Muhammad is both a prophet and a community leader. There is no division in Islam between "religion" and "politics", both are part of the way of life laid down by the Qur'an. The Prophet Muhammad and his successors were both religious and political leaders of the Muslim community and the Islamic state.

During his ten years in Madinah, Muhammad and the Muslims fought battles to defend themselves against the idol-worshippers of Makka. By the time that he died, most of the clans of the Arabian peninsula had come under his rule and most had embraced Islam as a way of life, although those who were Christians and Jews were permitted to practise their faith and were protected by the Muslim army.

During these years, after the death of his first wife in 621 CE, Muhammad contracted twelve marriages with women from various Arab clans. Sometimes these were political unions to cement good relations with a particular clan and sometimes they were acts of kindness to take in and care for a widow whose husband had been lost in battle.

The Qur'an permits a Muslim man to marry up to four wives, provided that he can treat them all equally, but the case of Muhammad was a one-off exception in order to provide practical guidance on how to treat all sorts of women fairly.

Reading the Qur'an

As has already been said, the Qur'an is literally the Word of God sent down in Arabic into the heart of the Prophet and from there it was proclaimed by his lips, then memorised and written down by his companions. It is divided into chapters, called *suras*, and verses, called *ayat*. There are one hundred and fourteen chapters in all. They vary considerably in length from more than two hundred and fifty down to three verses. They are not arranged chronologically but generally the shorter later chapters of the Qur'an were the first to be revealed during the years in Makka. As the Qur'an was revealed in Arabic, technically speaking it cannot be translated. Any translation is an interpretation. It is like translating Shakespeare into another language; one might capture something of the meaning but the full force of the original is untranslatable. There are English versions of the Qur'an readily available. The best are those that have footnotes to explain the meaning of the text. Anyone wanting to read the Qur'an is best advised to work slowly through the second chapter looking carefully at the footnotes. This chapter touches on all the major themes of the Qur'an. To understand it properly is a work of great dedication involving the learning of Arabic and the study of the context into which each verse was revealed.

The Prophet Muhammad was, of course, the first and the best commentator on the meaning of the Qur'an. Muhammad was given a special purification through an infusion of knowledge direct from God. This meant that there was no sin in his life. Everything that Muhammad said, did and approved of became a living commentary on the Qur'an. The life of Muhammad is an example of the perfect living out of the Qur'anic message. His teaching and actions were recorded in thousands of traditions, called Hadith, which were memorised by his companions and later written down to form the best guide to living out the message of the Qur'an.

The Islamic Empire

By the time that Muhammad died in 632 CE, nearly all of the Arabian peninsula was under the rule of Islam. There followed one of the most rapid expansions in all history. By the year 637CE, the Islamic Empire had spread to Palestine and Iraq; by 641 to Egypt and Syria, and by 650 to the ancient kingdom of Persia. Within eighty years, the Islamic Empire had spread as far as north India in the east and Morocco in the west. In 714 CE, it crossed into Spain and by 756 almost the whole of Spain was under Muslim rule. It is important to note here that there is a difference between the expansion of the Islamic Empire and conversion of people to become Muslims. Like any other empire, this one was spread by the conquests of the army, but people were not converted to Islam so quickly. Many, as in Egypt, Syria and Iraq, remain Christian up to the present time. Others gradually converted to Islam over a period of several generations.

The example of Islamic Spain is very important for us in Europe and the West today. During the Golden Age of Islamic Spain from 756 to 1036 CE, Jews, Christians and Muslims lived in peace under an Islamic government. Arabic was the common language of scholarship and the learned of all three religions worked side by side to push forward the frontiers of knowledge. It was at this time that the wisdom of ancient Greece, now in Arabic translation, returned to Europe after the Dark Ages. It was eventually translated into Latin, which was the academic language of Northern Europe. This was a time of great progress in mathematics, chemistry, medicine, algebra, astronomy and philosophy.

There were dark aspects of this relationship too. The Crusades from 1095 to 1291 left a terrible scar on Christian – Muslim relations. In a more positive way, at the very same time, Muslims, Jews and Christians of Toledo in Spain were doing the work of translation inspired by Peter the Venerable, the abbot of the great monastery of Cluny in France, who died in 1156. This was also the time that Francis of Assisi (d. 1226) was alive and trying to bring his message of peace between the Crusaders and Muslim armies in the Holy Land.

Jihad

We often hear about Jihad in Islam and sometimes people call this the "Holy War". Jihad actually means to struggle and strive on God's path to establish goodness and justice and to root out evil and oppression. In Islam there are two kinds of Jihad: the Greater and the Lesser Jihad. As its name suggests, the Greater Jihad is the more important. This is the constant struggle in the life of every Muslim to root out everything in their lives that is sinful or in rebellion against the way of life that God intends for us.

The Lesser Jihad is to take up arms to defend oneself, or the oppressed, or to preserve the Islamic way of life if it is under attack. Islam is not a pacifist code of living. If there is no alternative and everything else has been tried, then it is permitted to fight in the cause of right. This is always a war of self-defence against oppression. Strict laws of engagement were laid down in the earliest centuries of Islam. War must never be waged indiscriminately. Women, children, the elderly and infirm, and all non-combatants must not be attacked or threatened. It is forbidden to deprive an enemy of the basic means of survival; so water sources must not be poisoned, food crops must not be burnt and even trees must be spared as they provide fuel and shelter. Religious buildings and those who are inside them must not be attacked. Only the minimum force necessary must be deployed. Within these guidelines, if there is no other course of action, the legitimate leader of the Muslim community may call a Jihad and then all Muslims are expected to take part if necessary.

One Islam but many schools of thought

Whilst Islam is one and Muslims form a single community of believers living according to the guidance of the Qur'an and the example of the Prophet, there exist many different schools of thought within this one community. The earliest divisions came about concerning the succession after Muhammad as leader of the Muslim community. One party believed that the Qur'an and Muhammad had indicated that his successors had to come from the family of the Prophet. They backed Ali, the cousin and son-in-law of Muhammad, and parted company with the majority of the Muslim community. This party was called the Shi'a (Party) of Ali and forms the Shi'a Muslims today, who are concentrated in Iran and Iraq, and many are found in the Lebanon, the Gulf States and Pakistan.

The majority group, today comprising about 90% of all Muslims, became known as the Sunnis because they said that they followed the *Sunna* or example of Muhammad's life and teaching. They are to be found in almost every country around the world. The Sunnis also contain different schools of thought based on the different ways in which the Islamic way of life was drawn up into codes of practice by the early scholars. These various codes agree on all essential points but differ on details. This codification of the Islamic way of life is called the *shari'ah*, which covers every aspect of life: politics, economics, worship, family life, education, community building and business practices.

Over the course of 1400 years, both Sunni and Shi'a groups have developed many movements and sub-groups, which bring richness and diversity within the ultimate unity of the worldwide Muslim community. The important thing has always been the quality of the lives of those inspired by the guidance of the Qur'an and the example of the Prophet. The initial phase of expansion through the Muslim army was never repeated. Islam spread to the non-Arab world through the example of traders who took it along the Silk Road into China, throughout the Spice Islands of Indonesia and along the coast of East Africa. Most of the Muslims of West Africa, Malaysia and Central Asia owe their conversion to Islam to the pious example of Sufi Muslims, who were inspired by the mystical dimensions of Islam. Today there are around one billion Muslims worldwide. There are more Muslims in Indonesia than in all the Arab lands put together.

We all remember that during the last few centuries, the European nations colonised many parts of the world. This meant that the vast majority of Muslims were living under European colonial rule. During recent decades, this colonial rule has been thrown off and many new Muslim nations have come into being. The humiliation and exploitation of colonialism have left their mark on the Muslim world. Muslims were promised in the Qur'an that they would always enjoy the favour of God, so what happened? Why is it that many Muslims are amongst the earth's poorest peoples? Why is it that Muslims were largely left behind by the industrial and technological revolutions? Many in the Muslim world feel a kind of crisis. They say to themselves, "If only we had been better Muslims, then the favour of God would not have passed from us." The decision of these people is to return to the fundamentals of Islam and to try to get Muslims to practise their Islam in every aspect of life. A tiny minority become unbalanced and extreme in their views and so become the Muslim extremists about whom we read in the press. The vast majority are sincerely dedicated to living a life based on the balanced principles and thus seeking the pleasure of God.

Principal beliefs of Islam

The principal beliefs of Islam are condensed from the teaching of the Qur'an and the Prophet and drawn up into creeds or statements of belief. The starting point is always the absolute oneness of God who has no partners and does not share divinity with any creature. The essence of God is unknowable as our human language and knowledge cannot reach into God's world. We can speak about God according to the ways that God works within the creation. Thus we can call God the Merciful, the Compassionate, the Just, the Creator, the Guide, the Sustainer, the Truth, the First and the Last and so on. All these are names of God that are found in the verses of the Qur'an. There are ninety-nine such names and each tells us something about God. You may have seen Muslims with a string containing ninety-nine beads called a *tasbih*. One use for a *tasbih* is to remember the 99 Beautiful Names of God and thus to meditate on each of these qualities. One of the goals of a Muslim life is to take on as much of each of these qualities in one's own life as possible so that each Muslim becomes thus more God-conscious.

Angels are an essential aspect of Muslim belief because they are the agents of God who bring messages to this earth and do God's will in all things. They have no free will and so are inferior to human beings, who can freely choose to bring their lives into harmony with the will of God. An angel brought the message which was contained in the books or scriptures to the earth for the guidance of human beings. These books were given to the prophets who taught them to people and lived them out in practice. It is required that all Muslims believe in all the prophets sent by God and all the books that were revealed. In this way, a Muslim must believe in the prophethood of Moses and Jesus, for example.

God decided to give human beings free will so that we might be accountable for our deeds. God knows everything and is not limited by time, so God knows how we will use our God-given powers of free will. However, the responsibility for all our acts is ours alone. We will be held to account for all that we have done and failed to do at the final judgement at the end of time. This judgement is to be held in awe as Muslims believe that we will all appear individually before God as Judge. Those judged righteous on that day will go to Paradise for all eternity but the alternative is the torment of Hell.

The principal practices of Islam

The goal then of a Muslim life is to live a happy, prosperous and balanced life here on earth in such a way that one will be judged worthy of a place in Paradise at the end of time. All the practices of Islam are elements of training to lead the believers to this two-part goal. It is said that Islam is like a building that stands on five pillars. These five pillars are the five principal practices of Islam.

1. *Shahada*. To profess the principal creed of Islam.
2. *Salah*. To keep up the regular practice of formal prayer.
3. *Zakah*. To purify one's economic life by Islamic principles.
4. *Siyam*. To fast during the month of Ramadan.
5. *Hajj*. To make the pilgrimage to Makka once in one's lifetime.

The fifth pillar has already been covered when we were speaking about Abraham and Ishmael, so we will deal now with the first four.

Shahada

The principal creed of Islam reads: "There is no god, i.e. nothing worthy of worship, save God. Muhammad is the Prophet of God." To profess this creed publicly before two witnesses makes one a Muslim. The creed is in two parts. The first is a reminder of the absolute oneness of God but also warns Muslims to allow nothing to come in the way of their worship of God alone. Traditionally this might have been the old idols that the Arabs in the time of Muhammad worshipped. Idolatry, though, can take many forms. It might be that one places intermediary "idols" between oneself and God or it may be that one "worships" power or money or prestige and allows this to come in the way of the worship of God. The second part brings the abstract into a reality. It is only through the prophets of God, and especially Muhammad about whose message Muslims can feel certain, that one knows anything about God and so can worship God alone.

Salah

All Muslim adults are required to break off from their normal daily routine five times each day to offer their formal prayers to God. This is a command from God and so to obey it is good for people, even if one does not understand fully at the present moment. This formal prayer brings one into the closest attitude of submission to the will of God. Here the believer is alone and yet joined to all Muslims worldwide in humble prostration before the Creator. This is the moment of mercy and forgiveness. Because the five prayers take place at set times during the day, regulated by the passage of the sun, there are never more than a few hours between times of prayer. Any turning away from the straight path of harmony with God can be brought before God in humble submission now and forgiveness sought. It is as though at these times of prayer a river of mercy flows from God's world into which believers dip themselves to be restored and purified once more to engage in the world of work. Verses from the Qur'an are recited during these prayers and these provide guidance for the whole of life, so that life is fed by the times of prayer.

The Muslim is expected to pray before sunrise, shortly after midday, after the middle of the afternoon, directly after sunset and at night-time. Prayer can be offered in any clean place but there is an increased blessing if one prays in congregation with others. One may pray at home, in the office, at work, at school or there may be a place set aside for communal prayers such as a mosque or prayer room in another building. It is normal to make this prayer place particularly clean and fitting by spreading a carpet or cloth of some sort. Each prayer is to be offered in the direction of Makka. God is not in any one place, of course, but this earthly focus reminds individual Muslims that they are not alone but are joined with fellow believers who turn towards the same place from all over the world. Thus Makka is like the hub at the centre of a wheel with spokes radiating to every part of the globe.

Before beginning to pray, the Muslim must be physically and ritually or spiritually clean. The former is achieved by taking a shower or washing as necessary. The latter is achieved by a ritual washing of the hands, arms, mouth, nose, ears, head and feet. As one washes each part, the Muslim recalls and asks forgiveness for any sins that might have been performed by these parts of the body. This is called *wudu* and may be performed at home before prayers or in the washrooms of a mosque, if one is to pray there. Having achieved physical and ritual purity, the next thing is to purify one's inner self by making a declaration of intention to offer the appropriate formal prayer.

Each formal prayer consists of a number of cycles: 2, 3 or 4. A cycle is made up of a series of bodily postures, recitation of verses from the Qur'an and phrases uttered in praise of God. The cycle begins with standing upright in total concentration on God. Then verses from the Qur'an are recited in Arabic. The Muslim responds to the guidance of God by making a profound bow and saying "All glory be to God". Then one straightens, kneels and goes into the first of two prostrations in which the forehead and hands are placed on the floor in total submission to God. The Muslim then kneels up and the prostration is repeated. During this time one repeats pious expressions in Arabic such as "God is the Greatest". After the final prostration, one remains kneeling, repeats the *shahada*, invokes God's blessings on Muhammad and his family as well as on Abraham and his family, and then stands. Thus one cycle is completed. At the end of each time of prayer, greetings of peace are exchanged with the whole of creation to one's right and one's left. There may then follow informal personal prayers asking blessings from God that can be offered in any language and using whatever words the Muslim might choose.

In Islam, no one stands between the believer and God. Each Muslim has direct access to God without the need for any intermediary. Prayers in congregation are led by an imam, who is chosen as the most knowledgeable and pious Muslim man present. In a mosque, there may well be someone appointed to act as imam for the five daily prayers. The principal prayer of the week takes place on Friday shortly after midday. Friday is not "a day of rest" for Muslims but men are expected to leave off their work for sufficient time to bathe themselves and take part in the Friday Prayers. Women are free to attend these prayers but are not obliged to do so. A particular duty laid upon Muslim women is to establish the regular routine of prayers at home to sanctify it and to introduce younger children to the rhythm of prayer. Part of the Friday Prayers is an address given by someone who is knowledgeable about Islam. It will apply some element of Islamic teaching to any aspect of the life of those present. Thus it could as well be about community order, politics, world affairs, economic life or family responsibilities as about the celebration of a festival or an aspect of religious life.

Zakah

Often the Qur'an links together the regular prayers and paying the *zakah* as the two poles of establishing a Muslim way of life. *Zakah* is hard to translate accurately. It is an essential part of the whole Islamic economic system which is based on the principle of "bearing one another's burdens". If another human being is in need, then it is my problem and something about which I should do whatever I can.

This bearing of one another's burdens means, for example, that money can never be hoarded in an Islamic economic system but must be put to good use for the benefit of all. There is nothing wrong with being rich or investing for one's future or for the upkeep of one's family but any form of economic exploitation is against the code of Islam.

Islam forbids usury as a form of economic exploitation. The scholars may dispute the precise meaning of the term in the modern world but it is generally taken to mean the giving and taking of interest on a loan. If I lend someone a sum of money at interest and secure my loan against that person's home, then I am sure of the return of my capital plus interest even if the person goes bankrupt as my capital, secured against the borrower's home, is privileged over the borrower's labour and business endeavour. This would be a form of exploitation. Similarly an interest system is always inflationary. If I borrow at ten percent, then I must inflate the cost of my products by at least ten percent to bring in the return to cover the cost of the interest. Instead, Islam prefers a profit-sharing basis for raising capital by which I inject capital against a predetermined share of the profits (or the losses if they ensue). This tends to make the lender somewhat more responsible in financial transactions.

It is against this whole context that *zakah* must be placed. It requires that people assess their surplus wealth each year, that is what remains after basic living costs have been paid, and identify two and a half percent of it as no longer belonging to them but rather belonging to those who need it as *zakah*. Similarly, *zakah* is paid on other forms of wealth at various rates. This *zakah* must then be used for set purposes:

- To bring relief to the poor and needy
- To allow slaves to buy their freedom or to ransom prisoners of war
- To relieve the burdens of debtors
- To assist those suffering financial hardship because of becoming Muslims
- To help travellers who are stranded
- To spread the message of Islam
- To support those who administer the *zakah* funds.

Each individual adult Muslim is responsible for correctly assessing their payment of *zakah*. Each must see that the money reaches the appropriate people. Some people will know family and friends in need of *zakah*, others will give it to a reliable charity to distribute on their behalf. In an Islamic State, this task would be done by an office of the government.

Hospitality to travellers, welfare to those in need, setting up hospitals and schools, and taking care of widows and orphans have all been very important in Muslim societies. It is all part of belonging to one common humanity. The economic principle of this worldwide community is "to bear one another's burdens".

Siyam

Ramadan is the ninth month of the Islamic calendar and is set aside as a month of fasting. Throughout the month, every adult Muslim, with certain exceptions like the sick, the traveller, the elderly and pregnant or nursing mothers, must abstain from all food, drink and marital relations during daylight hours. What is the point?

To begin, let us go back to the principle that the Creator knows what is best for the creation. The fast during Ramadan is commanded by God and therefore it must be good for human beings. Food, drink and sex are all good things in Islam and they are permissible for Muslims during the hours of darkness during Ramadan. Fasting is not about torture, it is about self-control. The human urges to eat, drink and have sex are amongst the strongest we have. If we can learn to control these during daylight hours for a month, then we will gain control over every aspect of our lives. Fasting is a kind of training to make us more human by being in control and being able to survive when trials come upon us.

Every day around the world, thousands of people die of hunger and thirst. By feeling just a little of their suffering it reminds us of our duty to do something about it. Fasting is an act of solidarity with the poor. We all take food and drink for granted but we would have none of it if it were not for the providence of God and the efforts of those who grow and process our food. Fasting helps us not to take this for granted. Fasting changes the sugar levels in our blood and so makes it easier to "rise up" from an obsession with our earthly life by focussing on spiritual practices.

Ramadan is not just a time of negatively "giving up" things, it is also an opportunity to be more particular about prayers and reading the Qur'an. Many Muslims follow the pious tradition of listening to or reciting the whole of the Qur'an during the month of Ramadan. In many mosques and homes, people gather each night to pray and listen to one-thirtieth of the Qur'an being recited, so that the whole Qur'an is heard in the course of the month. Finally, Ramadan provides the opportunity to review and consider many other aspects of life. There is the "fasting of the tongue": do we gossip, tell lies or use bad language? There is the "fasting of the eyes": do we look at things and entertain thoughts that are bad for us? There is the "fasting of the hands": do we earn and spend our money in proper ways?

Ramadan is the holiest month of the year because it is the month in which the first revelation of the Qur'an took place. This event is celebrated on the Night of Power, which is one of the odd-numbered nights towards the end of the month, normally the 27th. On this night it is customary for Muslims to spend many hours in prayer asking for the mercy and blessings of God.

Ramadan ends with a feast: 'Id al-Fitr, the Feast of Fast-breaking. On this day, Muslims gather in the biggest mosques in each place to pray and give thanks for the blessings received during the fasting month. Before going to pray, each household must make a gift to the poor to make sure that everyone is able to celebrate the festival. A special meal is prepared and shared with family and friends. Gifts are exchanged, especially new clothes, and everyone is dressed in their best to make a round of visits.

Living constantly remembering God

We began this booklet by trying to sum up Islam in one sentence and all else has been working out what that means. To be a Muslim is to be fully engaged in human life. There are no monks in Islam; to be married and raise a family are important parts of the Muslim way of life. To be a Muslim is to be conscientious in following the prayers, fasting and economic system as a training in a godly life. To be a Muslim is to follow the guidance of God in every aspect of life so that every thought and action serves as a constant reminder of our standing before God.

God is the Creator and designer of the whole of creation. When all human beings, by obeying the revelation and imitating the Prophet, live in perfect harmony with the Creator and the rest of creation, then there is perfect happiness in this life and the prospect of unending joy in the life to come. This is the essence of Islam.

FURTHER READING

1. **Ahmed, Akbar S:** *Living Islam: from Samarkand to Stornoway.* London, Penguin, 1993

2. **Armstrong, K:** *Muhammad – A Western Attempt to Understand Islam.*
   London, Victor Gollancz Ltd., 1992

3. **Cohn-Sherbok, D[ed]:** *Islam in a World of Diverse Faiths.* New York, St. Martin's Press, 1991

4. **Cragg, Kenneth:** *The Event of the Qur'an: Islam and Its Scripture.*
   Oxford, One-World Publications, 1994

5. **Endress, G:** *An Introduction to Islam.*
   Edinburgh, Edinburgh University Press, 1988

6. **Haleem, Harifya A[ed]:** *Islam and The Environment.* London, Ta Ha Publishers Ltd. 1998

7. **Jomier, J:** *How to Understand Islam.*
   London, SCM, 1989

8. **Lings, M:** *Muhammad: His Life Based on the Earliest Sources.* London, George Allen and Unwin, 1983

9. **Momen, Moojan:** *An Introduction to Shi'i Islam.*
   New Haven, Yale University Press, 1985

10. **Nasr, Seyyed Hossein:** *Ideals and Realities of Islam.* London, Unwin, 1988

11. **Rahman, Fazlur:** *Islam.* Chicago, Chicago University Press, 1979

12. **Rahman, F:** *Major Themes of the Qur'an.*
    Minneapolis [USA], Bibliotheca Islamica, 1980

13. **Robinson, Neal:** *Islam: a concise introduction.*
    London, Curzon, 1999

14. **Sarwar, G:** *Islam: Beliefs and Teachings.*
    3rd Edition, London, Muslim Educational Trust, 1984

15. **Schimmel, A:** *Mystical Dimensions of Islam.*
    Chapel Hill [USA], University of North
    Carolina Press, 1975

16. **Sherif, Faruq:** *A Guide to the Contents of the*
    Qur'an. Reading, Garnet Press, 1995.